I0410899

Rural Development Provisions in the 2014 Farm Bill (P.L. 113-79)

Tadlock Cowan
Analyst in Natural Resources and Rural Development

September 4, 2014

Congressional Research Service

7-5700

www.crs.gov

R43718

Summary

While many legislative proposals introduced in a given Congress may have implications for rural America, Congress has generally expressed concern with economic development of rural communities within the context of periodic omnibus farm bills, most recently in Title VI of the Agricultural Act of 2014 (P.L. 113-79). Congress uses farm bills to address emerging rural issues as well as to reauthorize and/or amend a wide range of rural programs administered by the U.S. Department of Agriculture's (USDA) three rural development mission agencies: Rural Housing Service, Rural Business-Cooperative Service, and Rural Utilities Service.

Title VI of the 2014 farm bill addresses a wide range of policy issues concerning rural America, many of which were also addressed in the 2008 farm bill. These issues included provisions such as equity capital development in rural areas, regional economic planning and development, essential community facilities, water and wastewater infrastructure needs, value-added agricultural development, and broadband telecommunications development. The 2014 farm bill expands high-speed broadband access in rural areas through a new rural gigabit network pilot program, establishes new criteria for prioritizing broadband loans, creates a new rural energy savings program, establishes a program for strategic economic and community development, and consolidates several existing business development grants into a broader program of business development grants. The bill also authorizes $150 million in mandatory spending for pending rural development loans and grants, primarily water and wastewater infrastructure projects. A side-by-side comparison of the final bill with the House- and Senate-passed provisions is provided at the end of the report.

The 2014 farm bill authorizes USDA to prioritize otherwise eligible applications that support multijurisdictional strategic economic and community development. The provision reserves 20% of a fiscal year's appropriation for community facilities, water and wastewater projects, and rural business development for such strategic economic development projects. The bill authorizes a new Rural Energy Savings Program that will provide 0% interest rate loans to eligible borrowers to implement energy efficiency measures. The bill also authorizes appropriations of $10 million annually (FY2014-FY2018) for a new Rural Gigabit Network Pilot program for "ultra-high speed" broadband connectivity, and amends through FY2018 many long-standing programs funded through annual appropriations—water and waste disposal grants, technical assistance for rural water systems, emergency community water assistance, business opportunity grants, water assistance to Native villages in Alaska, community facilities for tribal colleges, and distance learning and telemedicine, to name a few. Most of these programs received authorized funding at levels generally lower than authorized by the 2008 farm bill.

Contents

Appendixes

Contacts

Policy Background and Overview

While farm commodity issues may occupy center stage in policy discussions of the periodic omnibus farm bills, rural community and economic development are also topics of congressional concern and are a separate title within the farm bill. Since 1973, omnibus farm bills have included a rural development title. The most recent is Title VI of the Agricultural Act of 2014 (P.L. 113-79). Positioning rural areas to better compete in a global economic environment is one of the key issues framing the current debate about the future of rural America. When agricultural production and related businesses dominated rural economies, policies that strengthened and improved agriculture tended to strengthen and improve the well-being of most of America's small communities and rural residents. As the strength of this linkage has declined, the need for new sources of rural economic development has become more apparent to policymakers and rural development practitioners.

Congressional interest in rural policy encompasses a wide range of issues, including agriculture, forestry, and mining; community infrastructure; natural resource conservation and management; medical care; bioenergy; and economic development. Current challenges to and reform of existing federal rural policies are evolving in an environment of increasing concern about economic competitiveness, a shift away from agriculture toward services, and new federal political strategies. A changing rural America is also producing pressures for different policies and raising new questions about what Congress's role should be in shaping rural policy.

Both agriculture and manufacturing issues are increasingly regarded as elements of global and regional restructuring, which have significant implications for rural areas, especially those areas where these production sectors remain dominant. Today, over 90% of total farm household income comes from off-farm sources.[1] The service sector, as with the U.S. domestic economy as a whole, now dominates the rural labor market, although the rural service sector differs from the metropolitan service sector in terms of job categories, skills, and wages.

The rural development title of farm bills generally supports (1) the infrastructure of rural areas, with traditional assistance for housing, electrical generation and transmission, water and wastewater, and community capacity; (2) agricultural development; and (3) rural business creation and expansion. More recently, policymakers have pushed for programs that support innovative and alternative business development, and new mechanisms to finance it. Pressure for such alternative approaches is expected to continue as policymakers recognize the changing structure of agriculture and the great diversity among rural communities, with some rural areas growing and prospering, and others falling further behind as their primary industries (including agriculture) either decline or adapt to a global economy. Such adaptation and dislocation over the past decade has often meant fewer rural employment opportunities and significant population outmigration for many rural communities.

To emphasize the importance of agricultural production in the local economies that still characterize many rural areas, legislative support for technologies to help farmers with planting decisions and local investments in industries that will add value to their products have become important aspects of rural development policy. Research is also increasingly focused on

---

[1] This figure reflects the significant proportion of small, "lifestyle" farms whose owners are not primarily involved in production agriculture. For those farms where agricultural production is central to the household's income, the proportion of off-farm income is less.

improvements in agricultural waste management and environmental protections. Traditional strategies, notably value-added agriculture (e.g., regional food processing plants, cooperatives, organic farming, biofuels) are being promoted by many in the farm sector. While these strategies hold promise for agriculture and surrounding communities, there remain limits on the extent to which agriculture and other mature industries can become a significant engine for renewed rural economic prosperity.

While commodity policy dominates much of the debate and most of the funding in the farm bill, production agriculture remains a comparatively small and shrinking part of the rural economy, with less than 8% of the rural population employed in agriculture. There is growing recognition that farmers in many rural areas depend more on a healthy rural economy than the rural economy is dependent on farmers for its vitality. The need to strengthen the capacity of rural areas more generally to compete in a global economy is becoming more widely appreciated as the limitations of commodity subsidies, peripheral manufacturing, and physical infrastructure as mainstays of rural development policy become more obvious.

Issues Influencing the Rural Development Title

The policy debate focuses on the question of whether current farm policies, which rely heavily on commodity support payments and subsidies to a few production sectors, help, hinder, or have little impact on the future development of economically viable rural communities. Rural manufacturing, which tends to be lower-skilled and lower-waged, is also undergoing restructuring with the loss of manufacturing to foreign competition. While transformation to a service economy continues in rural America, service employment in many rural areas tends to be in lower-wage personal services rather than business and producer services. Continuing population and economic decline in many farming and rural areas is compelling policymakers and rural areas to create new sources of competitive advantage, innovative ways of providing public services to sparse populations, and new ways of integrating agriculture into changing rural economies.

More recently, economic development efforts in some areas have targeted various entrepreneurial strategies and microenterprise development. These approaches attempt to capitalize on a particular area's distinctive social, economic, and environmental assets and advantages to build endogenously on existing local and regional strengths. Developing a local and regional entrepreneurial culture seems to be an important approach in these efforts' successes. Linking public and private sources to build "business incubators" is a common strategy, as is developing new commercial ties with area colleges and universities. Communities are also applying such entrepreneurial energy to making their local governments, schools, and hospitals more efficient through, for example, telecommunication innovations.

The trends noted above suggest a range of issues that were important in shaping the provisions of the rural development title of the 2014 farm bill:

- conservation and environmental restoration as rural employment opportunities;

- stemming rural population out-migration;

- vertical integration and coordination of agriculture into supply networks and their implication for rural areas;

- developing rural entrepreneurial capacity;

- rebuilding an aging rural physical infrastructure;

- public service delivery innovations in sparsely populated areas;

- increasing suburbanization and the conflicts between agriculture and suburban development;

- human capital deficiencies in rural areas;

- regionally based efforts for economic development; and

- connecting businesses and rural communities with broadband telecommunications infrastructure.

The rural development title of the 2014 farm bill took shape against this backdrop of shifts in the rural economy, widespread and long-term poverty in some rural areas, outmigration in other rural areas, dwindling economic opportunity in rural areas, gaps in critical infrastructure, and a growing appreciation in many quarters of the limits of existing rural development programs to respond to the great diversity of rural places and socioeconomic circumstances.

Federal Rural Development Programs

More than 88 programs administered by 16 different federal agencies target rural economic development. The Rural Development Policy Act of 1980 (P.L. 96-355), however, named USDA as the lead federal agency for rural development. USDA administers most of the existing rural development programs and has the highest average of program funds going directly to rural counties (approximately 50%).[2] Three agencies are responsible for USDA's rural development mission area: the Rural Housing Service (RHS), the Rural Business-Cooperative Service (RBS), and the Rural Utilities Service (RUS). An Office of Community Development provides community development support through Rural Development's field offices.

It is important to note that most loan and grant programs administered by USDA Rural Development are funded through annual (discretionary) appropriations. The rural development title of omnibus farm bills does not address every program administered by the three USDA mission agencies. Many of these programs are "permanently" authorized, often through amendments to the Consolidated Farm and Rural Development Act of 1972 (the ConAct, P.L. 87-128) or the Rural Electrification Act of 1936, and are funded through annual appropriations. Farm bills generally give the authority to appropriate discretionary funds for these "permanently" authorized programs for specific time, usually for the authorized period of the farm bill.

Title VI of the Agricultural Act of 2014 (P.L. 113-79)

While there have been long-standing arguments for the need to address the unique issues facing rural America through a comprehensive rural policy, the unique needs and resources of very different rural areas and the absence of any nationally organized rural constituency make that an unlikely outcome in the near term. Congress has chosen instead to address national rural policy

---

[2] More information on individual USDA Rural Development programs and funding levels can be found in CRS Report RL31837, *An Overview of USDA Rural Development Programs*, by Tadlock Cowan.

issues in this and most previous farm bills, through support for a portfolio of loans, loan guarantees, and competitive grant programs that generally address three major deficits that most all rural areas experience: (1) rural infrastructure, (2) rural business development and retention strategies, and (3) rural investment capital. The three mission agencies of USDA Rural Development support such a policy, with their respective emphasis on housing and community facilities, water, broadband, and electrical generation, and business/cooperative development. While local rural economic development is shaped by the distinctive resources that different rural areas can draw on, infrastructure, business planning and development, and the general absence of capital are three clear needs that virtually all rural areas can identify. The nearly 60 different loan and grant programs currently administered by USDA Rural Development generally follow this agenda. Newly authorized programs in the 2014 farm bill, as with previous farm bills, have reinforced this emphasis.

In the 2014 and the 2008 farm bills, newly authorized programs that address rural development issues from a regional perspective, as opposed to a local emphasis alone, have become more prominent. In addition to the authorization of three new regional development commissions in the 2008 farm bill, the 2014 farm bill also prioritized multijurisdictional planning for strategic rural development. These regional efforts suggest some movement away from the very local, *ad hoc* needs of rural communities, and toward a more comprehensive planning approach that, in time, could begin to shape the contours of a more comprehensive national and integrated rural policy.

Below, the various provisions of the 2014 rural development title are briefly outlined. An **Appendix** provides a complete side-by-side comparison of current law with the provisions of the House and Senate bills and the final enacted bill.

New Provisions in the 2014 Farm Bill

Concerns about how effectively USDA targets its rural development loan and grant assistance have been a recurring consideration by policymakers and rural development practitioners. The general concern is that rural development funding may not be targeted as well or as effectively as it could be. Section 6209 directs USDA to begin collecting data regarding economic activities created through USDA Rural Development grants and loans, and to measure the short- and long-term viability of award recipients. The provision also directs USDA to submit a report every two years with information on rural employment generation, new business start-ups, and any increased local revenue.

The rural development title authorizes a new Strategic Economic and Community Development initiative (Section 6025) that will prioritize projects that support economic development plans on a multijurisdictional basis. Other criteria for project selection include planning developed through the collaboration of multiple stakeholders in the service area of the plan, including the participation of combinations of stakeholders such as state, local, and tribal governments, nonprofit institutions, institutions of higher education, and private entities. Priority is also given to projects with investment from other federal agencies, and philanthropic organizations. The program reserves 10% of the appropriation for community facilities, rural utilities, rural business and cooperative development accounts for projects that meet the criteria of strategic development.

Other new provisions in the rural development title include the following programs:

- Section 6015 creates a new **Rural Business Development Grants** program. The program essentially terminates the Rural Business Enterprise grant program and the Rural Business Opportunity grant program and combines their general functions into the new grants program. It has an authorized appropriation of $65 million annually FY2014-FY2018, subject to annual appropriations. This authorized annual funding level is substantially more than the two grant programs it replaces.

- Section 6014 reauthorizes loans and loan guarantees for **locally or regionally produced agricultural food products**—those products that travel less than 400 miles between production and marketing. The program targets low-income areas without access to fresh fruits and vegetables. An increase of up to 7% of the appropriation for the Business and Industry Loan Guarantee program is authorized. Funding priority is given to projects benefitting underserved communities (i.e., those with limited access to affordable, healthy foods and with high rates of poverty or food insecurity).

- Section 6002 eliminates the reserve funding under the **Community Facilities** grant program for child care facilities.

- Section 6205 authorizes a new **Rural Energy Savings Program.** The program provides loans to utility districts and Rural Utility Service borrowers to assist rural households and small businesses in implementing durable, cost-effective energy efficiency measures. The program has an annual appropriation authorization of $75 million annually for FY2014 through FY2018, subject to annual appropriations.

- Section 6105 authorizes a new **Rural Gigabit Network Pilot Program** (operating at a 1 gigabit per second downstream transmission capacity) that could bring ultra high-speed broadband to more rural areas. The program has an annual appropriation authorization of $10 million each year for FY2014 through FY2018.

- Section 6006 authorizes an **Essential Community Facilities Technical Assistance and Training Program.** This grant program provides public entities and nonprofit corporation the technical assistance and training necessary to prepare reports and surveys necessary to request financial assistance under the Community Facilities loan and grant program. The program will also provide training to assist in the management of community facilities. Funding for the program comes from a 3%-5% carve-out of the funds appropriated for the Community Facilities loan and grant program.

- Section 6208 modifies the definition of "rural area" for the **Housing Act of 1949**. The provision increases the maximum eligible population threshold to 35,000 from 25,000 and permits any rural area that was eligible in the 1990, 2000, and 2010 census to remain eligible for Rural Housing Service programs until the 2020 decennial census.

Other Major Provisions

In addition to these newly authorized programs, the rural development title also includes other provisions to reauthorize and/or amend a wide variety of loan and grant programs that provide further assistance in four key areas: (1) broadband and telecommunications, (2) rural water and wastewater infrastructure, (3) business and community development, and (4) regional development. Each of these programs has authorized discretionary spending subject to annual appropriations, with the exception of one mandatory spending authorization of $150 million for reducing the backlog of pending water and waste water applications.

Broadband and Telecommunications

- Section 6104 reauthorizes the **Access to Broadband Telecommunications Services in Rural Areas**. The program was originally authorized in the 2002 farm bill (Section 6103) and funded by mandatory authorization. Its effectiveness, however, was limited by difficulties in implementation. The provision establishes new criteria for applications, reporting requirements, and prioritizing loans, which includes applications that provide broadband not primarily for business service if at least 25% of the customers in the proposed service territory are commercial interests. The provision also establishes minimum levels of downstream transmission capacity.

- Section 6201 reauthorizes the **Distance Learning and Telemedicine Loan and Grant Program,** which provides funding for end-user telecommunications equipment. The provision also emphasizes library connectivity as an objective of program funding. Funding is authorized at $75 million each year for FY2014 through FY2018, subject to annual appropriations.

Rural Utilities Infrastructure

- Section 6003 reauthorizes the **Rural Water and Wastewater Circuit Rider Program**, which provides technical assistance to rural water systems. Funding is authorized at $20 million annually (FY2014-FY2018), subject to annual appropriations.

- Section 6007 reauthorizes the **Emergency and Imminent Community Water Assistance Grant Program**, which provides funding to rural communities facing threats to the provision of potable water. Funding is authorized at $30 million annually through 2018, subject to annual appropriations.

- Section 6008 reauthorizes **Water Systems for Rural and Native Villages in Alaska**. Funding is authorized at $30 million annually through 2018, subject to annual appropriations.

- Section 6009 reauthorizes grants to nonprofit organizations for the construction and refurbishing of **Household Well Water Systems**. The program targets well systems for low-income individuals in rural areas. Authorized funding was reduced from $10 million to $5 million each year for FY2014 through FY2018, subject to annual appropriations.

- Section 6210 provides $150 million in mandatory funding for **Pending Water and Wastewater Loan and Grant Applications.** This would be a one-time expenditure designed to remove some of the current backlog of applications.

Business and Community Development

- Section 6005 reauthorizes **Tribal College and University Essential Community Facilities** through 2018. This program targets funding under the Community Facilities Program. Essential facilities include those that support public safety infrastructure and provide community health care.

- Section 6013 reauthorizes **Rural Cooperative Development Grants**. This provision permits multi-year grants (up to three years) for awards to rural cooperative centers. It provides a 20% set-aside for rural centers working with socially disadvantaged communities when the appropriation level exceeds $7.5 million. It provides an appropriation of $40 million each year for FY2014 through FY2018.

- Section 6023 reauthorizes the **Rural Microentrepreneur Assistance Program.** Funding is authorized at $3 million annually through FY2018. The program provides loans and grants to third-party organizations to assist small businesses that cannot otherwise get credit at reasonable terms. The third-party entities provide expertise to the small businesses in developing and implementing innovative projects.

- Section 6015 reauthorizes the **Appropriate Technology Transfer for Rural Areas Program (ATTRA)**. The program supports a cooperative agreement between the Rural Business-Cooperative Service and the University of Arkansas to provide information and technical support for sustainable and organic agricultural production. Authorizes $5 million annually through FY2018, subject to annual appropriations.

- Section 6203 reauthorizes the **Value-Added Agricultural Market Development Program**. This provision targets funding for "mid-tier value chains" which are local and regional supply networks linking independent producers with businesses and cooperatives. It also reserves 10% of the Value-Added Products Grants for projects benefitting beginning or socially disadvantaged farmers and ranchers. Funding is authorized at $63 million annually (FY2014-FY2018), subject to annual appropriations. The measure also prioritizes loans that contribute to opportunities for beginning farmers and ranchers, socially disadvantaged farmers or ranchers, and small and medium-size family farms.

- Section 6028 reauthorizes the **Rural Business Investment Program** through FY2018. This program was authorized in the 2002 farm bill and provides capital for Rural Business Investment companies, which, in turn, make loans to start-up businesses. The purpose of the program is to create a funding source for venture capital in rural areas. The reauthorization provides a total of $20 million each year for FY2014 through FY2018, subject to annual appropriations.

Regional Development

- Section 6026 reauthorizes the **Delta Regional Authority**, a federal-state partnership serving a 240-county/parish area in an eight-state region of the Mississippi Delta region. Section 6024 authorizes $3 million annually through FY2018 for grants to support health care services, health education programs, health care job training programs, and development and expansion of public health-related facilities in the Delta region.

- Section 6027 reauthorizes the **Northern Great Plains Regional Authority (NGPRA)**, a regional economic planning and development commission that supports regional infrastructure and business development in Iowa, North and South Dakota, Minnesota, and Nebraska.

- Section 6206 directs the Secretary of Agriculture, in coordination with the Secretary of Transportation, to conduct a **Study of Rural Transportation Issues** regarding the movement of agricultural products, renewable fuels, and economic development in rural America.

- Section 6207 reauthorizes funding for three new regional economic development and infrastructure commissions created by the 2008 farm bill: **(1) the Northern Border Regional Commission; (2) the Southeast Crescent Regional Commission; and (3) the Southwest Border Regional Commission.** Funding is authorized at $30 million annually through FY2018 for each commission, subject to annual appropriations.

Appendix. Side-by-Side Comparison of Rural Development Provisions in the 2014 Farm Bill with the House- and Senate-Passed Farm Bills

Prior Law/Policy—Rural Development	Senate-Passed 2013 Farm Bill (S. 954)	House-Passed 2013 Farm Bill (H.R. 2642)	Enacted 2014 Farm Bill (P.L. 113-79)
Consolidated Farm and Rural Development Act (ConAct) Authorizing statute for USDA's rural development programs. [7 U.S.C. 1921 et seq.]	Reorganizes the Consolidated Farm and Rural Development Act (ConAct). Consolidates rural development programs, makes technical changes to various programs, eliminates programs, establishes criteria for prioritizing loan and grants, eliminates the definition of "rural" and "rural area" for water assistance and community facilities. Makes technical changes to the Delta Regional Authority and the Northern Great Plains Regional Authority. [Sec. 6001] **Note: References below cite the new numbering of the ConAct for provisions notably amended by the Senate bill, followed in bold by the section of S. 954 making the change.**	No comparable provision.	No comparable provision. ConAct is not restructured.
Defining Rural Eligibility			
Sec. 343(a)(13)(A) of the Consolidated Farm and Rural Development Act (ConAct), as amended, defines rural as any area other than a city or town with a population greater than 50,000 and the urbanized area contiguous and adjacent to such a city or town.	Retains Sec. 343 (a) definition of rural as any area other than a city or town with a population greater than 50,000 and the urbanized area contiguous and adjacent to such a city or town.	No change to current law.	No change to current law.
Defines rural and rural area for water and waste water programs as any town, city, or unincorporated area under 10,000 population.	Eliminates the rural definition for water and waste water projects so that the definition above applies. Areas that were eligible for water and waste water funding under the prior definition will remain eligible for funding unless USDA determines that the area is no longer "rural in character."	No change to current law.	No change to current law.
Defines rural and rural area for community facility loan and grant program as any area other than a	Eliminates the rural definition for community facility loan and grants so that	No change to current law.	No change to current law.

Prior Law/Policy—Rural Development	Senate-Passed 2013 Farm Bill (S. 954)	House-Passed 2013 Farm Bill (H.R. 2642)	Enacted 2014 Farm Bill (P.L. 113-79)
town or city with a population greater than 20,000. Establishes criteria for determining areas as "rural in character" and makes certain exclusions for rural areas that could be classified as lying within an "urbanized area." [7 U.S.C. 1991(a)(13)(A)]	the definition above applies. Areas that were eligible for community facility funding under the prior definition will remain eligible for funding unless USDA determines that the area is no longer "rural in character." Amends criteria for determining areas "rural in character" and establishes priorities in making these determinations. Extends the current exclusion for "urbanized areas" where a single road may cause a rural town to be included within an urbanized area. Section 3002 28(A)(i) of the ConAct. [Sec. 6001]	No change to current law.	No change to current law.
Definition of Rural Area for Purposes of the Housing Act of 1949. Section 520 of the Housing Act of 1949 defines "rural area" as any area so defined between 1990 and 2000 to remain so classified until receipt of the 2010 decennial census. The provision also caps the eligible rural population threshold at 25,000 residents or less. [7 U.S.C. 1490]	Amends Section 520 of the Housing Act of 1949 to define a "rural area" as any area deemed to be a "rural area" at any time between January 1, 2000 and December 31, 2010 to continue to be so classified until receipt of data from the 2020 decennial census. Raises the eligible population threshold of a rural area to a maximum of 35,000 residents. [Sec. 6202]	No comparable provision.	Same as the Senate provision. [Sec. 6208]
Rural Community Programs			
Rural Water and Waste Disposal Loan and Grant Programs. Loans and grants to support improvements to rural water systems. Authorizes $30 million in grants annually FY2009-2013, subject to annual appropriations. [7 U.S.C. 1926(a)(2)	Reauthorizes funding to make loans, grants, and loan guarantees for the Rural Water and Waste Disposal Loan and Grant Programs. Establishes priorities for rural water programs, including a priority for rural communities of 5,500 or fewer permanent residents. Section 3501 (a)-(d)(f) of the ConAct. [Sec. 6001]	Reauthorizes the Rural Water and Waste Disposal Loan and Grant Programs. Decreases the current authorization for grants from $30 million to $15 million each year for FY2014-FY2018. [Sec. 6001]	Reauthorizes the Rural Water and Waste Disposal Loan and Grant Programs. Retains the current authorization of appropriations at $30 million each year for FY2014-FY2018. [Sec. 6001]
	No comparable provision.	Amends the water and waste water direct and guaranteed loan programs to encourage financing by private or cooperative lenders to the maximum extent possible; by using loan guarantees where the population exceeds 5,500; by	Same as the House provision. [Sec. 6019]

Prior Law/Policy—Rural Development	Senate-Passed 2013 Farm Bill (S. 954)	House-Passed 2013 Farm Bill (H.R. 2642)	Enacted 2014 Farm Bill (P.L. 113-79)
		using direct loans where the impact on rate payers would be significant if a loan guarantee were to be used; by requiring projects that require interim financing in excess of $500,000 initially to seek funding from private or cooperative lenders; and determining if an existing direct loan borrower can refinance with a private or cooperative lender prior to providing a new direct loan. *[Sec. 6015]*	
Revolving Funds for Financing Water and Waste Water Projects Program. Provides capital to fund revolving loan funds for supporting rural water projects. Authorizes $30 million annually for 2008-2013, subject to annual appropriations. *[7 U.S.C. 1926(a)(2)(B)]*	Reauthorizes funding for Revolving Funds for Financing Water and Wastewater Projects at $30 million annually for FY2014-FY2018, subject to appropriations. Section 3501(e)(1) of the ConAct. *[Sec. 6001]*	No change to current law, including no extension of authorization to appropriate funds to the program.	No mention of the program in the conference agreement. Funding authority expires.
Emergency and Imminent Community Water Assistance Program. Provides assistance to rural communities of 10,000 or less where there is a threat to potable water supplies. Authorizes funding of $35 million for each fiscal year FY2008-2013. *[7 U.S.C. 1926a(i)(2)]*	Reauthorizes funding for Emergency and Imminent Community Water Assistance Program at $35 million annually for FY2014-FY2018, subject to appropriations. Section 3501(e)(2) of the ConAct. *[Sec. 6001]*	Reauthorizes funding for Emergency and Imminent Community Water Assistance Program. Decreases current authorization of $35 million to $27 million annually for FY2014-FY2018, subject to appropriations. *[Sec. 6008]*	Adopts the Senate provision authorizing appropriations of $35 million for each fiscal year FY2014-2018. *[Sec. 6007]*
Water and Waste Facility Loans and Grants to Alleviate Health Risks. Provides loan and grant support to rural water systems to improve sanitation and potable water supplies. Authorizes an annual appropriation of $30 million in loan subsidies, $30 million in grants, and $20 million in grants for Tribal groups. *[7 U.S.C. 1926c]*	Reauthorizes funding for Water and Waste Facility Loans and Grants to Alleviate Health Risks at $60 million in loan subsidies, $60 million in grants, and $20 million in grants specifically for Tribal groups annually for FY2014-FY2018, subject to appropriations. Section 3501(e)(3)(B) of the ConAct. *[Sec. 6001]*	No change to current law.	No change to current law *[Sec. 6008]*

Prior Law/Policy—Rural Development	Senate-Passed 2013 Farm Bill (S. 954)	House-Passed 2013 Farm Bill (H.R. 2642)	Enacted 2014 Farm Bill (P.L. 113-79)
Grants for Water Systems for Rural and Native Villages in Alaska. Funding for water projects to improve sanitation and potable water in rural Alaska. Authorizes $30 million annually for FY2008-FY2013, subject to appropriations. [7 U.S.C. 1926d]	Reauthorizes funding for the program and specifies eligibility for native villages for Alaska and Hawaii for Water and Waste Facility Loans and Grants to Alleviate Health Risks to include Native Tribes, rural or native villages in Alaska and Hawaii. Section 3501(e)(3)(B) of the ConAct. [Sec. 6001]	No change to current law, including no extension of authorization to appropriate funds to the program.	Same as the Senate provision. [Sec. 6008]
Solid Waste Management Grants. Provides grant assistance for communities to establish or improve solid waste management facilities. Subject to annual appropriations. [7 U.S.C. 1932(b)]	Reauthorizes funding for Solid Waste Management Grants at $10 million annually for FY2014-FY2018, subject to appropriations. Section 3501(e)(4) of the ConAct. [Sec. 6001]	No change to current law.	Same as the Senate provision. [Sec. 6011]
Rural Water and Wastewater Technical Assistance and Training Grants. Provides funding for technical and managerial expertise assistance from third parties (e.g., National Rural Water Association Program) to assist rural communities with various water and waste water issues. Authorizes that between 1% and 3% of total water and waste water appropriation be allocated to these grants annually for FY2008-FY2013. [7 U.S.C. 1926(a)(14)]	Reauthorizes funding for Rural Water and Wastewater Technical Assistance and Training Grants at the current allocation rate of between 1% and 3% of the total water and waste water appropriation annually for FY2014-FY2018. Section 3501(e)(5) of the ConAct. [Sec. 6001]	No change to current law.	No change to current law.
Rural Water and Waste Water Circuit Rider Program. Provides funding to support technical assistance to water rural water systems. [7 U.S.C. 1926(a)(22)]	Reauthorizes the Rural Water and Waste Water Circuit Rider Program. Authorizes funding of $25 million for FY2014 and each year thereafter, subject to annual appropriations. [Sec. 6001]	Reauthorizes the Rural Water and Waste Water Circuit Rider Program. Authorizes funding of $20 million for FY2014 and each fiscal year thereafter, subject to annual appropriations. [Sec. 6005]	Adopts the House provision authorizing $20 million each fiscal year, subject to annual appropriations, subject to annual appropriations. [Sec. 6003]
Special Evaluation Assistance for Rural Communities and Households (SEARCH) Program. Provides grant assistance to communities under 2,500 to help them prepare an application for a water or waste water loan and grant.	Reauthorizes funding for the SEARCH Program at such sums as necessary for FY2014-FY2018, subject to annual appropriations. Section 3501(e)(6) of the ConAct. [Sec. 6001]	No change to current law.	No change to current law.

Prior Law/Policy—Rural Development	Senate-Passed 2013 Farm Bill (S. 954)	House-Passed 2013 Farm Bill (H.R. 2642)	Enacted 2014 Farm Bill (P.L. 113-79)
Up to 4% of the funds appropriated for water and waste disposal projects and essential community facilities may be used to fund SEARCH grants. Authorizes funding not to exceed $30 million in any fiscal year. [7 U.S.C. 2009ee]			
Grants to Nonprofit Organizations to Finance the Construction, Refurbishing, and Servicing of Individually-Owned Household Water Well Systems in Rural Areas for Individuals with Low or Moderate Incomes. Provides funding to third-party organizations with expertise in residential well-water systems. Authorizes $10 million annually FY2008-FY2013, subject to appropriations. [7 U.S.C. 1926(e)]	No comparable provision.	Reauthorizes the Household Water Well Systems Program. Decreases current authorization of appropriations from $10 million to $5 million for each fiscal year 2014-2018. [Sec. 6009]	Adopts the House provision reducing the authorized funding to $5 million for each fiscal year 2014-2018. [Sec. 6009]
Community Facilities Loan and Grant Program. Provides loan, grant, and loan guarantees for "essential community facilities." Most funding has supported projects for improved community health and safety (e.g., health clinics, elder care facilities, fire protection, and emergency responders). Authorizes such sums as necessary annually, subject to appropriations. [7 U.S.C. 1926(a)(19)]	Reauthorizes funding for Community Facilities Programs at $10 million annually for FY2014-FY2018, subject to annual appropriations.	Eliminates the provision in current law that reserves 10% of Community Facility funds for child day care facilities. [Sec. 6003]	Adopts the House provision eliminating the 10% set-aside for child day care facilities. [Sec. 6002]
	Establishes new priorities for Community Facilities loans and grants, including prioritization for communities with less than 20,000 in population.	No comparable provision.	No comparable provision.
	Also authorizes a new Technical Assistance for Community Facilities Program as part of the current Community Facilities Program. Provides technical assistance and planning assistance to rural communities in developing essential community facilities. Reauthorizes such sums as necessary for FY2014-FY2018, subject to annual appropriations. Section 3502(a)-(d)(e)(g) of the ConAct. [Sec. 6001]	Reserves at least 3% and no more than 5% of the appropriation for Community Facilities to provide technical assistance for Community Facility projects. [Sec. 6007]	Conference substitute adopts the House provision and authorizes up to 5% of the Community Facilities Loan and Grant program for technical assistance to help smaller communities in the development of their applications to the program. [Sec. 6006]
		Directs the Secretary to use loan	Adopts the House provision authorizing

Prior Law/Policy—Rural Development	Senate-Passed 2013 Farm Bill (S. 954)	House-Passed 2013 Farm Bill (H.R. 2642)	Enacted 2014 Farm Bill (P.L. 113-79)
	No comparable provision.	guarantees in the Community Facilities program to the maximum extent possible. [Sec. 6004]	the use of loan guarantees for community facilities to the maximum extent possible. [Sec. 6004]
Tribal College and University Essential Community Facilities. Provides grant funding to entities that are tribal colleges to provide the federal share of the cost of developing specific tribal college or university essential community facilities. Authorizes funding of $10 million each fiscal year FY2008-2013. [7 U.S.C. 1926(a)(25)(C)]	Reauthorizes funding of $10 million each fiscal FY2014-2018, subject to annual appropriations.	Decreases the current authorization of appropriations from $10 million to $5 million each fiscal year 2014-2018. [Sec. 6006]	Adopts the Senate provision authorizing $10 million each fiscal year 2014-2018 subject to annual appropriations. [Sec. 6005]
Health Care Services. Addresses unmet health needs in the Mississippi Delta region through grants awarded to health care services and health care education programs. Authorizes $3 million appropriations each fiscal year FY2008-2102. [7 U.S.C. 2008u]	Reauthorizes the Delta Health Services program and authorization of appropriations. [Sec. 6001]	No comparable provision.	Adopts the Senate provision. [Sec. 6024]
Rural Business and Cooperative Development			
Rural Business Opportunity Grants. Provides grant assistance of up to $1.5 million to identify business opportunities that will use local rural resources, to train and provide technical assistance to existing or prospective rural entrepreneurs, to establish business support centers, and to support local and regional economic development planning. Authorizes $15 million annually for FY2008-FY2013, subject to appropriations. [7 U.S.C. 1926(a)(11)]	Eliminates the program, but consolidates its objectives within broad rural business development grants program. Authorizes $65 million annually for the broader program for FY2014-FY2018, subject to annual appropriations. Section 3601(a) of the ConAct. [Sec. 6001]	Authorizes $15 million annually for each fiscal year FY2013-FY2017. [Sec. 6002]	Concurs with the Senate provision to eliminate the program, but with several amendments. The amendment strikes Sections 310B(c) and 306(a)(11) in the Con Act and replaces them with the Rural Business Development Grant authority, allocating not more than 10% of amounts appropriated for the purposes previously authorized under the Rural Business Opportunity Grant authority. Combines two existing programs, the Rural Business Opportunity Grants program and the Rural Business Enterprise Grants program, into a single program to be known as the Rural Business Development Grants program, and authorizes $65 million for

Prior Law/Policy—Rural Development	Senate-Passed 2013 Farm Bill (S. 954)	House-Passed 2013 Farm Bill (H.R. 2642)	Enacted 2014 Farm Bill (P.L. 113-79)
			each fiscal year 2014-2018. [Sec. 6012]
Rural Business Enterprise Grants. Provides grant support of up to $50,000 to public bodies and nonprofit corporations for measures designed to facilitate small and emerging business enterprises, or the creation and expansion of rural distance learning networks, among other eligible activities. Authorizes funding not to exceed $50 million annually. Subject to annual appropriations. [7 U.S.C. 1932(c)]	Eliminates the program, but consolidates the program's objectives within a broad rural business development grants program. Authorizes $65 million annually for the broader program (as above) for FY2014-FY2018, subject to appropriations. Section 3601(a)of the ConAct. [Sec. 6001]	No change to current law.	Concurs with the Senate provision to eliminate the program, but with several amendments. The amendment strikes Sections 310B(c) and 306(a)(11) in the Con Act and replaces them with the Rural Business Development Grant authority, allocating not more than 10% of amounts appropriated for the purposes previously authorized under the Rural Business Opportunity Grant authority. Combines two existing programs, the Rural Business Opportunity Grants program and the Rural Business Enterprise Grants program, into a single program to be known as the Rural Business Development Grants program, and authorizes $65 million for each fiscal year 2014-2018. [Sec. 6012]
Value-Added Agricultural Product Market Development Grants. Provides grant support to agricultural producers to undertake projects that add value to commodities and thereby increase producer income. Also supports planning and business development for value-added projects. Authorizes $40 million annually FY2009-2013 subject to annual appropriations, in addition to $15 million in mandatory spending to remain available until expended. [7 U.S.C. 1621]	Reauthorizes funding for Value-Added Agricultural Producer Grants at $40 million annually for FY2014-FY2018, subject to annual appropriations. Also authorizes $12.5 million annually in mandatory spending for FY2014-FY2018. Establishes priority for projects in which at least 25% of the project recipients are beginning or socially disadvantaged farmers or ranchers. Section 3601(b) of the ConAct. [Sec. 6001] Amends Section 231(b) of the Agricultural Risk Protection Act of 2000 to give funding priority to, among other groups, veteran farmers and ranchers (as defined by the Food, Agriculture, Conservation and Trade Act of 1990). [Sec. 6207]	Reauthorizes the Value-Added Product Grant Program. Increases authorization of mandatory spending from $15 million to $50 million. [Sec. 6202]	Reauthorizes the program. Provides $63 million in mandatory spending and reauthorizes $40 million in annual appropriations though 2018. [Sec. 6203]
Locally or Regionally Produced Agricultural Food Products. Provides funding to increase domestic consumption of locally and regionally	Reauthorizes the program for FY2014-2018. [Sec. 6001]	Reauthorizes the program for FY2014-2018. Amends the provision so that not more than 7% of the funds of the Business and Industry Loan Guarantee program can	Same as the Senate provision. No other changes to current law. [Sec. 6014]

Prior Law/Policy—Rural Development	Senate-Passed 2013 Farm Bill (S. 954)	House-Passed 2013 Farm Bill (H.R. 2642)	Enacted 2014 Farm Bill (P.L. 113-79)
produced agricultural products and to provide affordable food products in underserved rural and urban areas. Reserves not less than 5% of the funds of the Business and Industry Loan Guarantee program for support of locally and regionally produced food. Requires an annual report to Congress on the program. [7 U.S.C. 1932(g)(9)(B)(v)(I)]		be used to fund locally or regionally produced agricultural food products. [Sec. 6012]	
Agriculture Innovation Center Demonstration Program. Provides grant funding to producers for technical assistance in developing agricultural-based businesses based on value-added production. Authorizes funding of $6 million annually for FY2008-2013, subject to annual appropriations. [7 U.S.C. 1632(b)(i)]	No comparable provision.	Decreases the current authorization of appropriations from $6 million to $1 million each fiscal year 2014-2018. [Sec. 6203]	Adopts the House provision reducing appropriations to $1 million each fiscal year 2014-2018. [Sec. 6204]
Rural Cooperative Development Grants. Facilitate the creation of jobs in rural areas through the development of new rural cooperatives, value-added processing, and rural businesses. Authorizes $50 million annually for FY2008-FY2013, subject to appropriations. [7 U.S.C. 1932(e)(5)]	Reauthorizes funding for grants at $50 million annually for FY2014-FY2018, subject to appropriations. Includes directive to coordinate an interagency working group among federal agencies to support cooperative development. Section 3601(c) of the ConAct. [Sec. 6001]	Decreases the current authorization of appropriations from $50 million to $40 million each fiscal year 2014-2018. [Sec. 6011]	Similar to the Senate provision, but authorizes $40 million in appropriations FY2014-2018. [Sec. 6013]
Appropriate Technology Transfer for Rural Areas (ATTRA). Provides grant support at an agricultural institution (e.g., universities) for information activities to agricultural producers. Authorizes $5 million annually for FY2008-FY2013, subject to appropriations. [7 U.S.C. 1932]	Reauthorizes funding for ATTRA at $5 million annually for FY2014-FY2018, subject to appropriations. Section 3601(d) of the ConAct. [Sec. 6001]	No change to current law, including no extension of authorization to appropriate funds to the program.	Reauthorizes ATTRA at $5 million annually FY2014-2018. Adopts the Senate provision, subject to annual appropriations. [Sec. 6015]

Prior Law/Policy—Rural Development	Senate-Passed 2013 Farm Bill (S. 954)	House-Passed 2013 Farm Bill (H.R. 2642)	Enacted 2014 Farm Bill (P.L. 113-79)
Business and Industry Loan Program. Provides loans for a wide variety of projects to support business development in rural areas and to increase and retain jobs in rural areas. Subject to annual appropriations. (Note: Direct loan program has not been funded since 2002.) [7 U.S.C. 1932(a)(2)(A)]	Reauthorizes funding of $75 million annually for FY2014-FY2018, subject to appropriations. Raises initial fee to 3% from current authorization of 2%. Reauthorizes a 5% carve-out of guaranteed loan authority for Locally or Regionally Produced Agricultural Food Products. Section 3601(e) of the ConAct. [Sec. 6001]	Reauthorizes program. Amends Section 310B of the ConAct to permit the Secretary to take a borrower's account receivables as security for Business and Industry loans and to permit working capital to be a loan purpose. Also requires the Secretary to promulgate regulations within 6 months to implement the changes authorized. [Sec. 6010]	Adopts the House provision permitting the financing of working capital to be a loan purpose, and encourages USDA to better coordinate with the Small Business Administration on outreach to rural lenders. [Sec. 6010]
Intermediary Relending Program (IRP). The IRP provides direct loans at 1% interest to intermediaries to finance business facilities and community development projects in rural areas of 25,000 population or less. The Rural Business Service loan to an intermediary is used to establish or fund a revolving loan program to provide financial assistance to ultimate recipients for community development projects, establishment of new businesses or expansion of existing businesses. Subject to annual appropriations. [7 U.S.C 1932]	Reauthorizes funding for IRP at $50 million annually for FY2014-FY2018, subject to appropriations. Section 3601(f)(1) of the ConAct. [Sec. 6001]	Reauthorizes and amends the program. Authorizes $10 million, subject to appropriations, for each fiscal year FY2014-2018. [Sec. 6013]	Reauthorizes the program and authorizes to be appropriated $25 million each fiscal year 2014-2018. Prohibits the Secretary from making loans under another authority (e.g., the Community Economic Development Act of 1981). [Sec. 6017]
Rural Microentrepreneur Assistance Program. Provides grant support to third-party entities that assist rural entrepreneurs in establishing microenterprises in rural areas. Authorizes $4 million in mandatory spending for FY2009-FY2011 and $3 million for FY2012. Also authorizes $40 million annually in discretionary spending for FY2009-FY2013, subject to appropriations. [7 U.S.C. 1981 et seq.]	Reauthorizes funding the program at $40 million annually for FY2014-FY2018, subject to appropriations. Also provides $3.0 million annually in mandatory spending for FY2014-FY2018. Section 3601(f)(2) of the ConAct. [Sec. 6001]	Decreases the current authorization of appropriations from $40 million to $20 million each fiscal year 2014-2018. [Sec. 6018]	Adopts the Senate provision authorizing mandatory spending of $3 million each fiscal year 2014-2018, and reauthorizes discretionary appropriations at current level of $40 million each fiscal year 2014-2018. [Sec. 6023]

Prior Law/Policy—Rural Development	Senate-Passed 2013 Farm Bill (S. 954)	House-Passed 2013 Farm Bill (H.R. 2642)	Enacted 2014 Farm Bill (P.L. 113-79)
Rural Business Investment Program. Modeled on the Small Business Administration's Small Business Investment Companies, the Rural Business Investment Program provides funding to help capitalized Rural Business Companies that, in turn, provide loans to rural businesses. Authorizes $50 million for the period FY2008-FY2013, subject to appropriations. Program was never implemented. [7 U.S.C. 2009cc et seq.]	Reauthorizes funding for the program at $25 million annually through FY2018, subject to appropriations. Provides authority for USDA to establish capital requirements, establish fees for applicants applying for a license to operate as a rural business investment company, and ensures the majority of capital of each rural business company is invested in rural concerns. Section 3602 of the ConAct. [Sec. 6001]	Decreases the current authorization of appropriations from $50 million to $20 million each fiscal year 2014-2018. [Sec. 6021]	Adopts the House provision decreasing appropriations to $20 million each fiscal year 2014-2018 [Sec. 6028]
Rural Business Collaborative Investment Program. Provides loan and grant support to rural regions to establish regional competitiveness by fostering collaboration among rural businesses, rural institutions, and entrepreneurs. Establishes multijurisdictional and multisectoral Regional Rural Investment Boards and provides Regional Innovation Grants. Authorizes $135 million for the period FY2008-FY2013, subject to annual appropriations. Program was never implemented. [7 U.S.C. 2009dd]	Terminates the program.	No change to current law, including no extension of authorization to appropriate funds to the program.	No change to current law.
General Rural Development Provisions			
General authority for USDA to award grants and to make and guarantee loans to various entities [7 U.S.C. 1926]	Reauthorizes and contains general provisions for loan and grant authority. Section 3701 of the ConAct. [Sec. 6001]	No change to current law.	No change to current law.
No comparable provision.	**Strategic Economic and Community Development.** Authorizes USDA to prioritize otherwise eligible applications that support mult jurisdictional strategic economic and community development and establishes criteria for evaluating	No comparable provision.	Adopts the Senate. [Sec. 6025]

Prior Law/Policy—Rural Development	Senate-Passed 2013 Farm Bill (S. 954)	House-Passed 2013 Farm Bill (H.R. 2642)	Enacted 2014 Farm Bill (P.L. 113-79)
	applications. Reserves 20% of a fiscal year's appropriated funds for rural community facilities, water and waste water projects, and loans and grants under Rural Business and Cooperative Development. Also reserves 15% of the total funds available for these functional categories for strategic economic and community development projects. Section 3703(a)of the ConAct. [Sec. 6001]		
Rural Development Loan Procedures. Addresses procedures for approving USDA Rural Development loans and grants. [7 U.S.C. 1983(a)]	No comparable provision.	Simplifies the loan application process. Directs USDA to provide a one-page application and other simplified application procedures. Within two years of enactment, requires USDA to submit a report to the House and Senate Agriculture Committees evaluating the implementation of this provision.[Sec. 6016]	Adopts the House provision. [Sec. 6020]
Rural Development Insurance Fund. Authorizes a revolving fund for the discharge of the obligations of USDA under contracts guaranteeing or insuring rural development loans. Funds not needed for current operations are deposited in the U.S. Treasury for credit to the fund, or invested in obligations guaranteed by the United States [7 U.S.C. 1929a]	Continues permanent authority for the Rural Development Insurance Fund. Section 3704 of the ConAct. [Sec. 6001]	No change to current law.	No change to current law.
Rural Economic Area Partnership (REAP). The program assists communities dealing with geographic and economic isolation, low density population, absence of nearby metropolitan centers, and historic dependence on agribusiness, out-migration, and economic upheaval to develop strategies for revitalization	Establishes process for USDA to designate new Rural Economic Area Partnership zones. Section 3705(a) of the ConAct. [Sec. 6001]	No change to current law.	No change to current law. [Sec. 6016]

Prior Law/Policy—Rural Development	Senate-Passed 2013 Farm Bill (S. 954)	House-Passed 2013 Farm Bill (H.R. 2642)	Enacted 2014 Farm Bill (P.L. 113-79)
Zones. [7 U.S.C. 1932]			
National Rural Development Partnership. A state-federal rural economic development coordinating entity operating through State Rural Development Councils and a National Rural Development Coordinating Committee. [7 U.S.C. 2008m]	State Rural Development Partnership. Establishes a federal-state partnership called the State Rural Development Partnership. The Partnership is composed of state rural development councils whose purpose is to build regional capacity in rural communities. The Partnership is designed to maximize public- and private-sector cooperation to minimize regulatory redundancy. The federal government will act as a partner or facilitator to provide states with technical and administrative support necessary to plan and implement rural development strategies tailored to meet local needs. [Sec. 6001]	No change to current law.	No change to current law. [Sec. 6021]
No comparable provision	No comparable provision	Rural College Coordination Strategy. Instructs the Secretary to develop a coordination strategy for USDA Rural Development programs to serve the specific needs of rural community and technical colleges. [Sec. 6014]	Adopts the House provision. [Sec. 6018]
No comparable provision.	No comparable provision.	Program Metrics. Directs USDA to begin collecting data on the economic activities created through its loan and grant funding. Specifically directs USDA to measure the short and long-term viability of award recipients, and to submit a report to Congress every two years on the actions taken to use the data, the number of jobs created, the value of wages, and other economic data deemed relevant. [Sec. 6204]	Adopts the House provision. [Sec. 6209]

Rural Telecommunications and Electrification: Rural Electrification Act

Rural Electrification Act of 1936. The act authorizes loans for rural electrification and telecommunications	No comparable provision	Relending for Certain Purposes. Amends the Rural Electrification Act to authorize loans for borrowers relending to	No comparable provisions.

Prior Law/Policy—Rural Development	Senate-Passed 2013 Farm Bill (S. 954)	House-Passed 2013 Farm Bill (H.R. 2642)	Enacted 2014 Farm Bill (P.L. 113-79)
infrastructure development. [9 U.S.C. 901 et seq.]	No comparable provision	ultimate consumers for the purpose of energy efficiency. Loans and grants are also authorized under the Cushion of Credit Payments Program for relending to ultimate consumers for the purpose of energy efficiency. [Sec. 6101] **Fees for Certain Loan Guarantees.** Amends the Rural Electrification Act to require that the Secretary, at the request of a baseload generation loan guarantee borrower, charge an upfront fee equal to the costs of the loan guarantee. A borrower may not use funds from a loan or other debt obligation made or guaranteed by the federal government to pay the fee. [Sec. 6102]	Adopts House provisions. [Sec. 6101]
Definition of Rural Area. Defines rural and rural area to mean any area other than a city or town or unincorporated place with a population greater than 20,000 residents, and any area within the service area of an electric, telephone, or telephone bank borrower under Section 13(3)the Rural Electrification Act. [7 U.S.C. 913]	Amends the definition of rural area for programs authorized by the Rural Electrification Act to be the same as the definition in Section 3002 (28)(A)(i): any area other than a city or town with a population greater than 50,000 and the urbanized area contiguous and adjacent to such a city or town. [Sec. 6101]	No change to current law.	Adopts the House provision; no change to current law defining rural for programs under the Rural Electrification Act. Not mentioned in conference agreement.
Rural Electrification Act of 1936. The act authorizes loans for rural electrification and telecommunications infrastructure development. [9 U.S.C. 901 et seq.]	No comparable provision	**Rural Utilities Service Contracting Authority.** Amends Section 18(c) of the Rural Electrification Act to insert a sentence that states that a contract funded by a borrower that is paid for out of the general funds of the borrower is not a public contract with the meaning of U.S.C. Title 41. [Sec. 6103]	No change to current law.
Guarantees for Bonds and Notes Issued for Electrification or Telephone Purposes. Provides for	Reauthorizes guarantees for bonds and notes issued for electrification or telephone purposes for 2014-2018. [Sec.	Identical to the Senate provision. [Sec. 6104]	Same as the House and Senate bills. [Sec. 6102]

Prior Law/Policy—Rural Development	Senate-Passed 2013 Farm Bill (S. 954)	House-Passed 2013 Farm Bill (H.R. 2642)	Enacted 2014 Farm Bill (P.L. 113-79)
federal guarantees for bonds and notes that finance rural electrification and telephone infrastructure. [7 U.S.C. 940c-1(f)]	6102]		
Expansion of 911 Access. Authorizes expanding the emergency telephone service of 911 in rural areas by using any funds otherwise made available for telephone loans for each of FY2008-FY2013. Section 315(d) of the Rural Electrification Act. [7 U.S.C. 940(e)d]	Reauthorizes expansion of 911 access through FY2018. [Sec. 6103]	Identical to the Senate provision. [Sec. 6105]	Same as the House and Senate bills. [Sec. 6103]
Access to Broadband Telecommunications Services in Rural Area. Provides loan guarantees to establish broadband telecommunications infrastructure in rural areas. Subject to annual appropriations [7 U.S.C. 950bb]	Reauthorizes funding for the program at $50 million annually for FY2014-FY2018, subject to appropriations. Amends Section 601 of the Rural Electrification Act to establish a grant component to the Broadband Loan Program. Establishes priorities for communities: (1) without a local service provider, (2) with populations of less than 20,000, (3) with a high proportion of low-income residents, and (4) experiencing significant out-migration. Also establishes a maximum grant limit of 50% of a project's development costs, but gives USDA the authority to increase the grant amount to 75% for remote communities and those with low-income residents. Also establishes priority to broadband applications that offer service to the greatest proportion of unserved rural households or rural households that do not have broadband service but meet the minimum acceptable levels of service. Priority would be given to communities with populations of 20,000 or less, or those experiencing outmigration, or those that are isolated from population centers, or those that have a high percentage of low-income residents. Also authorizes a	Reauthorizes the program through FY2018. Gives priority to applications that are not predominantly for business service but where at least 25% of customers in the proposed service territory are commercial interests. Publication of notice of applications shall include the amount and type of support requested and a list of the Census block groups or tracts to be served. The Secretary is authorized to establish a process where, at the time of an application notice, an incumbent service provider who is providing service to a remote rural area may submit to the Secretary information regarding the service offered in the application's proposed service area, so the Secretary may assess whether the application is an eligible project. The Secretary is also authorized to consider upgrade or replacement cost for construction or acquisition of facilities and equipment in considering the technology needs of customers in the proposed service area. [Sec. 6106]	Adopts the Senate provision with an amendment. The amendment requires USDA to establish at least 2 evaluation periods annually to compare applications to the program and set priorities, among other changes to the program. The amendment also requires USDA to establish a searchable database on the RUS website with information about applicants. Does not authorize a new grant program to accompany the existing loan guarantee program. [Sec. 6104].

Also authorizes the Rural Gigabit Network Pilot Program to provide loans and grants for high-speed service to rural areas, and authorizes appropriations of $10 million for each fiscal year 2014-2018. [Sec. 6105] |

Prior Law/Policy—Rural Development	Senate-Passed 2013 Farm Bill (S. 954)	House-Passed 2013 Farm Bill (H.R. 2642)	Enacted 2014 Farm Bill (P.L. 113-79)
	pilot program for "ultra-high speed" broadband connectivity. [Sec. 6104]		
Grants for NOAA Weather Radio Transmitters. Provides grant funding to public and nonprofit entities for the federal share of the cost of acquiring radio transmitter to increase coverage of rural areas by the all hazards weather radio broadcast system of the National Oceanic and Atmospheric Administration. Authorizes funding of such sums as necessary for FY2008-2013, subject to annual appropriations. *[7 U.S.C. 2008p]*	No comparable provision.	Authorizes $1 million each fiscal year 2014-FY2018, subject to appropriations. *[Sec. 6017]*	Adopts the House provision. *[Sec. 6022]*
Distance Learning and Telemedicine Program. Provides grants to rural hospitals, clinics, schools, and libraries to develop and improve their telecommunications infrastructure. Section 233A of the Food, Agriculture, Conservation, and Trade Act of 1990. Authorizes funding of $100 million annually through FY2013, subject to appropriations. *[7 U.S.C. 950aaa]*	Reauthorizes funding at current level through FY2018. *[Sec. 6201]*	Decreases the current authorization of appropriations from $100 million to $65 million each fiscal year 2014-2018. *[Sec. 6201]*	Authorizes appropriations of $75 million each fiscal year 2014-2018. *[Sec. 6201]*
	No comparable provision	In making awards under the program, the agency is directed to consider whether the applicant is located in a designated health professional shortage area, as defined in Section 332 of the Public Health Service Act. *[Sec. 6207]*	Does not direct the agency to prioritize applications in health professional shortage areas.
No comparable provision.	Amends Subtitle E of Title VI of the 2002 farm bill (P.L. 101-171) to authorize a new **Rural Energy Savings Program**, which would provide 0% interest rate loans to eligible Rural Utilities Service borrowers to fund loans to qualified consumers to implement energy efficiency measures. *[Sec. 6203]*	No comparable provision.	Conference agreement authorizes the Rural Energy Savings Program and authorizes $75 million to be appropriated $75 million each fiscal year 2014-2018. *[Sec. 6205]*
Backlog of Rural Development Applications. Section 6029 of the Food, Conservation, and Energy Act of 2008 (P.L. 110-246) provided a	Provides for one-time mandatory funding of $150 million for pending rural development loan and grant applications. *[Sec. 6204]*	No comparable provision.	Adopts the Senate provision providing $150 million in mandatory spending for pending rural development loan and grant applications. *[Sec. 6210]*

Prior Law/Policy—Rural Development	Senate-Passed 2013 Farm Bill (S. 954)	House-Passed 2013 Farm Bill (H.R. 2642)	Enacted 2014 Farm Bill (P.L. 113-79)
one-time $120 million in mandatory spending for pending rural development loan and grant applications. *[122 Stat. 1955]*			
No comparable provision.	**Study of Rural Transportation Issues.** Directs USDA and the Department of Transportation to jointly conduct a study regarding the movement of agricultural products, domestically renewable fuels, domestically produced resources for electricity production, and economic development for rural areas. Designates particular topics for the study to address. Study is to be updated triennially. *[Sec. 6205]*	Identical to the Senate bill, but also requires an update on the study to be submitted not later than 1 year after the date of enactment of this act. Also expands the study to include transportation infrastructure of water ways. *[Sec. 6205]*	Directs USDA and the Department of Transportation to jointly conduct a study of agricultural transportation needs, to include water infrastructure needs. *[Sec. 6206]*
No comparable provision.	Amends Section 203 of the Agricultural Marketing Act of 1946 (7 U.S.C. 1622) to direct USDA to participate on behalf of the interests of agriculture and rural America in all proceedings pertaining to freight rail policy of the Surface Transportation Board. *[Sec. 6206]*	No comparable provision.	Adopts the Senate provision. *[Sec. 6202]*
No comparable provision	No comparable provision.	**Certain Federal Action not to be Considered Major.** An action by the Secretary that does not involve the provision of federal dollars or a loan guarantee from USDA, including a debt settlement or restructuring, a lien accommodation or subordination, or the restructuring of a business entity by a borrower, in the case of a loan, grant, or loan guaranteed in the USDA Rural Development mission area, shall not be considered a major federal action. *[Sec. 6206]*	No comparable provision.

Regional Development Authorities

Delta Regional Authority. The Authority is an 8-state state-federal	Reauthorizes funding FY2014-FY2018 at the current level of $30 million annually.	Decreases the current authorization of appropriations from $30 million to $12	Adopts the Senate provision authorizing funding at $30 million each fiscal year

Prior Law/Policy—Rural Development	Senate-Passed 2013 Farm Bill (S. 954)	House-Passed 2013 Farm Bill (H.R. 2642)	Enacted 2014 Farm Bill (P.L. 113-79)
regional planning and development entity that provides loan and grant support for economic development projects in rural counties in the Mississippi Delta area. Authorizes $30 million annually for FY2008-2012 subject to appropriations. [7 U.S.C. 2009aa et seq.]	subject to annual appropriations. Also makes technical amendments to the operation of the Authority. Sections 3801 through 3814 of the ConAct. [Sec. 6001]	million each fiscal year 2014-2018. [Sec. 6019]	2014-2018, subject to annual appropriations. [Sec. 6026]
Northern Great Plains Regional Authority. Authorizes an economic development commission that develops regional plans and makes loans and grants for infrastructure and economic development in five Great Plains States. Authorizes $30 million annually for FY2008-2012, subject to appropriations. [7 U.S.C. 2009bb et seq.]	Reauthorizes funding FY2014-FY2018 at the current level of $30 million annually, subject to annual appropriations. Also makes technical amendments to the authority. Increases the cap on administrative expenses from 5% to 10%. Sections 3821 through 3835 of the ConAct. [Sec. 6001] NOTE: See also **Title XII-Miscellaneous, Section 12206,** for changes made in the Senate bill to other regional commissions authorized by the 2008 farm bill.	Decreases the current authorization of appropriations from $30 million to $2 million each fiscal year 2014-2018. [Sec. 6020]	Adopts the Senate provision reauthorizing current level of funding, but would require an annual audit only if funds are appropriated. [Sec. 6027]
Regional Economic and Infrastructure Development. The 2008 farm bill (Section 14217) established three new regional development authorities: a Northern Border Regional Commission, a Southeast Crescent Regional Commission, and a Southwest Border Regional Commission. These commissions develop a regional development plan and then make infrastructure loans and grants to eligible entities in their respective regions. [40 U.S.C. 15101 et seq.] Authorizes annual appropriations of $30 million to each of the Commissions. Not more than 10% of	Extends the authorization of appropriations through FY2018. Allows the cap on administrative expenses for any Commission to exceed 10% should the Commission receive an annual appropriation of less than $10 million. This provision is contained in the Miscellaneous title of the Senate bill. [Sec. 12206]	Same as the Senate provision. [Sec. 6208]	Same as the House and Senate bills. [Sec. 6207]

Prior Law/Policy—Rural Development	Senate-Passed 2013 Farm Bill (S. 954)	House-Passed 2013 Farm Bill (H.R. 2642)	Enacted 2014 Farm Bill (P.L. 113-79)
appropriated funds to any Commission can be used for administrative expenses. [40 U.S.C. 15751(b)]			

Author Contact Information

Tadlock Cowan
Analyst in Natural Resources and Rural
Development
tcowan@crs.loc.gov, 7-7600